D1794864

COUNSELLING...? ME?

COUNSELLING...? ME?

A Guide to the
Talking Therapies

Jonathan Ingrams

I'm all right but I'm not sure about him...

KARNAC

First published in 2011 by
Karnac Books Ltd
118 Finchley Road
London NW3 5HT

British Library Cataloguing in Publication Data

A C.I.P. for this book is available from the British Library

ISBN-13: 978-1-85575-871-1

Typeset by Vikatan Publishing Solutions (P) Ltd., Chennai, India

Drawings by Andy Hammond

Printed in Great Britain

www.karnacbooks.com

CONTENTS

ABOUT THE AUTHOR

Jonathan Ingrams came to counselling following twenty-five years of making medical educational programmes for doctors and general audiences in the United States and Europe. Over the past fourteen years he has practised as a psychotherapist with a broad spectrum of clients from the "worried well" to those suffering a range of mental illnesses of varying severity. His work has included counselling for Young Offenders and taking referrals from GPs, insurance companies, and Employee Assistance Programmes.

INTRODUCTION

ONE OF THE MAJOR problems for most of us when considering counselling is that we may have little or no idea what to expect. Given the multitude of ways this form of therapy is practiced and the jargon surrounding it, this is hardly surprising.

What, for example, is the difference between a psychiatrist and a counsellor? Or between a counsellor and a psychotherapist? Or a psychotherapist and a hypnotherapist? Or a hypnotherapist and an aroma therapist?

(For the record: A psychiatrist is a doctor trained to deal with mental illness and who may prescribe drugs; a counsellor is a consultant for personal problems. There is no formally recognized difference between a counsellor and a psychotherapist. A hypnotherapist will use hypnosis to treat persistent habits, typically

helping people who want to give up smoking. Aromatherapy involves the application of various oils to ameliorate psychological conditions. This may be combined with massaging and inhalation).

And which approach would best suit you? Freudian? Jungian? Rogerian? Psychodynamic? Transactional Analysis? Kleinian? Adlerian? Gestalt? CBT? REBT ...?

If you have to go to your doctor with a fractured wrist or a stomach upset, you have at least some idea of what sort of treatment to expect. But counselling? Is it just a chat between two people, one of whom calls him- or herself a counsellor (and charges a fee for it)? Or is there more to it than this?

There is an undercurrent of reporting that suggests that "talking therapies", as they are sometimes described, are being used too much as a catch-all coping strategy in any circumstances where someone might have had an uncomfortable experience or is at risk of undergoing one. For example, post traumatic stress disorder (PTSD), the term originally used to describe the psychological trauma experienced by troops who had undergone gruelling experiences in the front line of warfare, is now, especially for the purpose of claiming damages, routinely attributed to the most minor mishaps. Indeed, at the time a new Harry Potter book was about to be launched, one counsellor even advertised that she would offer therapy to children who may be traumatized by the content!

But there is solid evidence that psychotherapy, responsibly practiced, can be highly beneficial. For example, the army has expanded its access to counselling, having shown that it is effective in helping its troops deal with stress, and the availability of counselling in the NHS has greatly increased with additional government funding. Universities offer counselling on campus and many of the larger companies operate in-house counselling services, called Employee Assistance Programmes, (EAPs) to help members of staff who may be experiencing emotional problems.

The purpose of this short book is to help you decide on whether this form of therapy could be beneficial for you. It is daunting enough to contemplate sitting opposite a total stranger and imparting sometimes painful confidences to him or her. But if you know broadly what you can expect, the factors you should take into account before embarking on such a journey, and the part you will be expected to play, then you have a good chance of making a reasonably informed decision about what to do.

The book addresses twenty questions you might ask about counselling. Please be aware that it is not intended as a counselling manual, nor is it a lexicon of counselling methodology. I have endeavoured to give rounded answers to these questions so that the information in each section stands alone. As such, some themes and observations may be addressed in answers to other linked questions.

You may find the best way to use the content is to browse areas that interest you, then come back to review other aspects in your own time.

CHAPTER ONE

How do I know
if I might benefit
from counselling?

A KEY QUESTION, and not one with a simple answer. Counsellors advertise that they can help to resolve a range of difficulties; typically anxiety and stress, depression, work issues, loss of confidence, life changes, relationships and sexual problems, as well as more vaguely defined complexes such as "lack of purpose" or "deprivation". But how can you determine whether it might be useful for you to seek the services they provide?

A likely indicator is that you find yourself having persistent difficulty dealing with some aspect of your personal, social, or working life. Inevitably, there are periods when we all feel a bit down; sadness after a quarrel with someone we care about, disappointment that we didn't get the promotion we hoped for, annoyance because we think someone's behaved badly towards us, or regret if, on some occasion, we feel we haven't conducted ourselves as well as we would wish. This is the natural order of things. We make up after the quarrel, perhaps look for a better job, put aside the irritation we experienced, apologize to someone if we feel we need to—and move on.

But supposing, for reasons we may not fully understand, we find we can't "move on"? Some aspects of life we recognize that others seem able to manage with little difficulty become a major problem, putting us in a state of recurring anger, anxiety, or feelings of guilt. Situations that should be little more than mildly annoying may evoke gnawing resentment, or minor setbacks lead to deep depression.

The worst part of these feelings is the unproductive behaviour they induce. To avoid risking disapproval we may go to extravagant lengths to please. We may become obsessive about our health or impose unreasonable responsibilities on others to maintain our self-esteem. If we attend a job interview, believing that if we are not successful it is proof we're a failure, we're hardly going to present ourselves at our best. All these forms of thinking and behaviour are time-consuming, exhausting and, most importantly, act against our best interests.

One of the reasons that unhelpful patterns of thought or action persist is because we don't really know how they got there in the first place, and why we are perpetuating them. If we did, we might be in a position to do something about them. But we're not born with these difficulties. Unproductive ways of thinking, and the unhealthy emotions and conduct they generate, have been learned, often unwittingly, perhaps in earliest childhood. Importantly, the very fact they have been learned means they can be unlearned. This is where counselling can play a role. By helping us develop insight into the causes of our emotions and consequential behaviour, counselling can create the basis for us to adopt more productive ways of dealing with them. Counselling does not offer a cure like a medicine for an illness. The aim is to equip you with the knowledge and tools to become your own counsellor so that you can successfully address problems or difficulties that might arise even long after therapy has finished.

Bear in mind that counselling is not intended to resolve purely practical issues for which specialist knowledge is required; for example, difficulties you may be having in managing your finances, or where you are uncertain about your legal rights in a dispute. Under these circumstances it may be better to seek advice through an organization such as the Citizen's Advice Bureau, or to talk to an accountant or a solicitor. Significant addictions to alcohol or drugs dependencies are also best dealt with by specialists in these fields.

Going for counselling takes courage as it involves facing up to our difficulties and asking someone for help. It is tempting to believe that if we do this, it is evidence that we can't cope. In fact, the reverse is true. Making the decision to address our needs can be a major step forward in starting the coping process.

CHAPTER TWO

Do many people seek counselling?

MORE AND MORE of us do. Humans are best adapted to living in small units within an ordered structure, whose ethics and moral standards are accepted and followed by everyone. It was not so long ago that people in villages, or in largely self-contained communities in towns, would never feel the need to lock their cars or their doors when they went out. This is not to suggest that these were halcyon days, free of strife and danger. But social behaviour and customs reflected what was in the best interests of the community, and information from outside was restricted to what was needed for its survival and ongoing health.

Nowadays we live in an age of increasing pressure; pressure from information cascading in via television, radio, and the Internet; peer group pressure, both on ourselves and our children; pressure from advertising, from junk mail and from "phishing"; pressure to be politically correct, and from current obsessions over health and safety. Advertising, particularly on television, pursues a relentless goal of "happiness", portraying a picture of a world in which everyone can expect to be fulfilled by benefiting from the products and services being promoted. It is hardly surprising that sometimes this onslaught creates tensions that are tough to handle.

According to NHS statistics, one in four of us will have problems with our mental health at some time in our lives. Between 8% and 12% of the population experience depression in any year[1]. The UK has one of the highest rates of self-harm in Europe, at 400 per 100,000 population[2]. According to a recent survey, three-quarters of those questioned said that the world is a more frightening place than it was ten years ago[3]. The number of counsellors in Britain has tripled over the past decade,

---

[1] The Office for National Statistics Psychiatric Morbidity report (2001).
[2] Self-poisoning and self-injury in adults, Clinical Medicine.
[3] Mental Health Foundation.

just to keep up with demand. The government has set up a scheme, Improving Access to Psychological Therapies (IAPT) and announced additional funding to increase services over the next three years.

CHAPTER THREE

Why not just talk to a friend?

YOU MAY ASK yourself: What benefit is there in going through all your stuff with a perfect stranger when you can talk to people around you who care about you and know you well?

The problem with talking things over with family or friends is that usually they cannot, with the best will in the world, offer unbiased responses. In their desire to show sympathy, they may well contribute to the problem by reassuring you that your anger or anxieties are fully justified. "Sounds as if it's her fault, not yours". "That's terrible! He's no right to do that!". This may be what you want to hear, but if you unquestioningly go along with these justifications you are effectively letting others do your thinking for you. Importantly, you may not recognize what you may be contributing to the situation, or adjustments you could make in your thinking which would alter your perception of events.

Or, in wanting to demonstrate their psychological skills, friends or family may well jump in with judgements based on their views or experience, argue with your assumptions or offer simplistic solutions to the problem. They may be distracted by detail and pay more attention to the facts than the meaning they have

Getting help from a friend

for you. Paul Simon in his song *The Sound of Silence* talks of "hearing without listening", and in their eagerness to demonstrate their understanding, your friends may well launch into an event of their own, as in: "Tell me about it! I've been there—only for me it was even worse!" Before you know where you are, you're being hijacked into their stories.

You may also receive well-meaning recommendations such as: "Hey, you shouldn't worry so much!" "Don't take it to heart. It may never happen!" or more brutally: "Get a life!", "Chill out a bit!". The problem with this kind of advice is that it rarely comes with practical suggestions as to how to do these things. (Bear this knowledge in mind when you are talking to a counsellor. If you seem to be getting no more out of your sessions than you would from chatting to someone in the pub, they're not doing their job!).

CHAPTER FOUR

What does counselling set out to do?

ASKED WHAT they think happens in counselling, people will often describe it as having a chat with someone who will tell you what you've got wrong and give you advice or instructions on how to fix it. But counsellors never tell their clients—the term used to identify those coming for counselling—what to do. Just as well, if you think about it. The last thing we need is to find ourselves scurrying about trying to accommodate someone else's directions. Before long, we would find ourselves powerless to make our own decisions, devastated if we fail to meet their chosen agendas, and attached to them for life!

Counselling is about self-help; an active, collaborative process designed to enable you to explore unresolved issues in a secure environment and to better understand why they may be causing you difficulties. It can be bewildering trying to work out how one can have arrived at a particular and perhaps stubborn way of looking at things, particularly if the consequences are clearly unproductive. But the recall of life experiences is selective—it has to be or we'd be swamped with a mass of information, much of it irrelevant. Various emotional factors, or events we perceive as significant, influence what we store in our minds and what we delete from memory. Equally, however, there may be occasions where a crucial moment gets lost but the aftermath remains. A single incident of being bullied at school, perhaps long forgotten, can lead to an unconscious need to please as a form of self-protection which extends into adult life. A failure to make an impact on someone we wanted to impress as a child can lead to the concept that if someone rejects us there must be something wrong with us.

If we were brought up having to look after younger siblings or an elderly relative, which may have entailed often having to put their interests ahead of our own, we may have unwittingly persisted with this attitude, feeling we should always first meet other people's real or anticipated needs. In the process we become deprived of opportunities to move forward for ourselves. We may also develop feelings of entitlement, becoming angry if we do someone a favour which is not reciprocated in full. Emotions and beliefs we carry with us do not necessarily stem only from childhood. The breakup of a relationship, or loss of a job, may impact on confidence in other, unrelated, areas.

We may sometimes feel we are bound to respond to situations in the way we are doing. A troubled childhood in which our energies had to be focused on staying out of harm's way, or seeking to please in order to avoid punishment, can well give rise to a ongoing belief of being without options. Part of the objective of counselling is to help us understand the links between past events and present behaviour and to recognize that if, in the past, it seemed we had no choices, now we do; and that we can accept ourselves for who we are, rather than basing our value on the inferred judgments of other people.

Counselling is about change; changing from ways of thinking and acting that are not working for you, and may be holding up your life, to the adoption of courses of action that enable you move forward. Whether you may be concerned with specific problems, or coping with more broadly based, long-term issues, counselling sets out to enable you to see more clearly what is going on and to increase your awareness of yourself, your situation, and the choices that are open to you. It is no part of counselling to make you dependant on the therapist. The counsellor is not there to be a friend, nor to provide simple fixes or soft options. Working together as a team, the objective is to help you recognize the contribution you may be making to the problems you are experiencing and to find your own solutions, so that ultimately you become, in effect, your own counsellor. The process for doing this is reviewed in later chapters.

CHAPTER FIVE

Does counselling work?

ALTHOUGH FIRM STATISTICS are hard to come by, the answer must be "yes", as so many people, on their own admission, have benefited from it. The number of qualified counsellors has tripled in the last ten years to keep up with demand, and the government is investing some £400m to be used over the next three years to help improve psychological therapies. It has been shown in several studies that counselling can offer a useful alternative or supplement to drugs designed to alleviate anxiety or depression.

But if we ask whether counselling works, there is also the need to define "work". Counselling isn't like having a massage where we sit back while someone else rolls up their sleeves and makes all the running. Its success is highly dependant on the amount of commitment the person concerned is prepared to bring to the process and their willingness to keep an open mind to new ideas and ways of thinking.

It is important also to recognize that counselling doesn't effect a cure like an antibiotic with a bacterial infection. The counsellor's first objective is to create an environment in which you can gain an understanding of the thought processes that have given rise to the difficulties you've been experiencing. You should then be in a position, with the right support, to work towards making the changes that will enable you to better manage these. This calls for patience as well as endurance. Life perspectives you want to change or modify may have developed over many years and cannot realistically be displaced in a few weeks. Even when counselling has finished, you will still need to be aware of situations, and your response to them, that may previously have been problematic. The difference is that you should now be able to handle these situations so that you take control before they get out of hand.

CHAPTER SIX

How secure
is counselling?

FOR COUNSELLING to be effective, it is essential you feel able to discuss your concerns in the certain knowledge that what you say will be confidential. If you have any doubts about security, you will inevitably start to withhold information that could be important to your progress. For this reason the strictest confidentiality is rigorously observed and is fundamental to the requirements of all the professional counselling organizations.

Confidentiality isn't just a matter of the counsellor not revealing to anyone else their client's name; it means ensuring they avoid any comment or observation that might conceivably enable a third party to work out who that person might be. This can be particularly important in smaller communities where there is a greater likelihood that an injudicious remark could lead to someone drawing their own conclusions as to who is the other party.

Approach *not* practised by counsellors!

The only recognized exceptions to confidentiality are if a counsellor has strong evidence that a client may be about to harm themselves or another person, in which case they may want to contact their GP or other authority. But they should explain this at the start of therapy and never take such steps without their client's knowledge.

Your counsellor will usually assure you of confidentiality without prompting; if not, ask, emphasising that your commitment is dependant on this. Notes will usually be taken during sessions, but clients should be identified in them only by first names and sometimes just by a number. Professional ethics require that personal details should always be kept under lock and key.

CHAPTER SEVEN

How much does it cost?

COUNSELLING IS AVAILABLE free of charge on the NHS. But the maximum number of sessions normally allowed is six, which is unlikely to be sufficient unless there is just one specific, relatively straight-forward matter to be addressed. Also, there is usually a long waiting list that may run into months. Some of the larger companies will have employee assistance programs (EAPs) which either operate in house or are made available from outside counsellors. Sessions are usually free of charge for the member of staff concerned.

The alternative is to go through an agency or an individual independent counsellor. There are agencies with charitable status that may be able to offer counselling for a reduced fee according to an individual's means, but otherwise one should expect to pay from £30 to £45 a session. When debating whether to make this investment, it is worth considering what might be the emotional and practical costs of doing nothing. Also, whilst free counselling may seem the obvious option, the payment of a fee perhaps creates a more even balance in the relationship. Whilst one party has the specialist knowledge, the authority to engage them for the services they offer rests firmly with the other, as evidenced in the fee paid.

A final point; as the counsellor sets time aside specifically for you, she or he is likely to expect payment if you cancel the session, especially at short notice. It is important to ensure at the start of counselling that there is clear understanding of the arrangements for fees, the number of sessions contracted and the dates and times you will be meeting.

CHAPTER EIGHT

How long does it take?

THIS IS SOMETHING of a "piece of string" question. As the unfulfilled Alvy, in Woody Allen's film *Annie Hall*, decides after fifteen years on the psychiatrist's couch: "I'm going to give my analyst one more year and then I'm going to Lourdes!"

A number of factors will affect the overall time you spend in counselling. If you are experiencing difficulties in just one area in your life, then sessions are likely to be quite focused and results may be achieved sooner than if you need to address more complex matters. Single issues can be very stubborn, however, whilst seemingly intractable problems can sometimes take on the properties of a log jam in which the release of a one psychological obstruction can create beneficial knock-on effects across a broad spectrum.

The way your counsellor works can also affect the duration of therapy. Psychodynamic counselling, which aims predominately to bring to the surface painful feelings held deep in the unconscious mind, can be a long process. The cognitive behavioural therapies tend to focus on the here and now, and are more directive than other methods. Cognitive approaches are usually associated with shorter periods of therapy. But there are no rules, and all modalities now take into account that practitioners may have only a short period to work in.

It is worth asking counsellors how they practice even when you first make contact, so that you can assess whether the form of therapy they offer is likely to effective for you. After the initial sessions, your counsellor can probably give you some idea of how many he or she thinks may be necessary which, in turn, can be influenced by how they practice. You yourself should be able to gauge the progress you are making once counselling is under way. But bear in mind there will always be an element of discovery on both sides, and probably the best route is to agree an initial session to enable you both to decide whether future work together will be productive before making a further commitment.

Sessions usually run for between 50 minutes and an hour, and take place once weekly, although there may be exceptions in cases of particular need. If you opt to continue with therapy after the initial session, your counsellor may well propose a starting contract of around six sessions. This open structure allows you space within which to work without your feeling you have to reach a specific objective at the end of each session. Counselling is not a step-wise process and some sessions will inevitably be more productive than others. At the end of the contracted period your counsellor will usually review progress with you so that you can together decide on how best to proceed further.

It is important to recognize that your own commitment will have a significant impact on how long therapy needs to continue and how successful it will be. If you have agreed to have weekly sessions, missing the odd one might not seem too significant, but in many ways, counselling is like other forms of endeavour, such as a sporting activity or playing a musical instrument, where results depend not only on tutoring but on consistent and regular practice.

Even if you do regularly attend a weekly session but do no work on the issues in between, progress will be slow. Counselling involves change; change in the way you've been thinking, and changes brought about by your being able to talk things over with a professional. You will need to carry through what you learn about yourself to derive practical benefit. It is best to bring an agenda to sessions so that the work can be focused on aspects you most want to deal with. These may vary from week to week. Counsellors often encourage clients to keep a journal and to practice coping skills in situations they may previously have taken care to avoid. It is best to agree with your counsellor what you will try to achieve between sessions as counselling progresses, so that you don't attempt assignments that could be too difficult early on.

CHAPTER NINE

Where do I find a counsellor?

FINDING COUNSELLORS is the easy part. Look under "Counselling and Advice" in the local directories, and you will come upon as many as many as ten or fifteen practicing in your area, all of whom appear to offer help over a seemingly identical range of problems. So how do you find someone who could be suitable?

If you have major addictions, for example with alcoholism or drug taking, then you may be better advised to seek support from a specialist organization. AA (Alcoholics Anonymous) helps with significant drinking problems and there are substance abuse rehabilitation centres in various parts of the UK and Ireland, "Cruse" is a charity specializing in bereavement care; "Nexus" in sexual abuse and family support.

Sometimes partners in a relationship may consider the best approach is to consult someone who will see them together. The marriage council, now called Relate, is set up for couples counselling. Some private counsellors also specialize in specific areas and usually advertise accordingly.

Counsellors should be members of a professional body such as the British Association of Counselling and Psychotherapy (BACP), the British Association of Behavioural and Cognitive Psychotherapies (BABPC) or the UK Council for Psychotherapy (UKCP). These organizations have criteria for good practice and required levels of skill which can be identified on their websites.

Other factors include whether you would prefer to see a man or a woman. Women counsellors generally outnumber men. Ease of access is another consideration, but you may prefer to go to someone not in your immediate area, so reducing the likelihood that you will bump into your counsellor outside the counselling room. The relationship between client and counsellor is unlike any other and best contained strictly within the counselling environment.

Decide whether you are going to seek a practitioner via an agency or go to an individual. An advantage of going to an agency is that they are likely to have on their team counsellors who have come from a number of different backgrounds and whose experience and training give the agency as a whole a broad range of skills. Before assigning you a counsellor, the usual procedure is first to carry out an assessment. You will be asked why you have come for counselling, what your expectations are, and about any significant events that may have a bearing on how you look at life and how you are feeling now. You will also be asked about any experience you may have had with mental health services or previous counselling. The aim is to help determine whether counselling is right for you at this time, and to enable the agency to assign you to someone whose experience and way of working is most likely to produce results.

The atmosphere in an agency can sometimes feel less private than seeing an independent counsellor. If there is a waiting room, you may be aware of others coming for therapy. You will not previously have been able to talk to the counsellor you are assigned to, although you may be invited to express a preference for a man or a woman. If, after finishing counselling, you later decide you would like to return for further sessions it may not always be possible for you to see the same counsellor if the one you saw before has no free appointments.

Individual private counsellors usually have a preferred way of working according to their training and experience. Your initial selection will probably be guided by locality and even whether you like the look of the advertisement where you find their details. Unless you are convinced that the person you are speaking to seems right for you, tell them you will get back to them and move on to the second counsellor you have identified. In this way you should stand a fair chance of finding someone with whom you are likely to get on. Bear in mind, there will always be an element of discovery at the start of counselling, no matter whom you opt to work with.

CHAPTER TEN

How do I know who might be right for me?

THERE ARE NO GUARANTEES, but you can take steps to minimize the risk of a relationship that doesn't work. When you make contact, give the counsellor a very brief description of the issues you would bring to them such as "I am having difficulty controlling my temper" or "I find myself becoming anxious for no reason" and ask him or her how they would approach such a problem. A professional therapist should be able to give you a clear, intelligible reply. You might also ask when they last provided counselling for someone in a similar situation. The way questions like these are answered can be a useful indicator of a counsellor's skills in these areas.

The counsellor, too, is likely to ask you some questions, but don't expect a full consultation over the phone! From this initial discussion you should get some perception as to whether this is someone with whom you could productively share confidences. Feel free also to ask about their qualifications, which professional organization they're a member of, and how much experience they have. Experience is not just a matter of how many years a counsellor has been qualified, but how many hours he or she has actually worked with clients. Someone counselling for ten years but who sees only one or two clients a week will actually have far less experience than someone seeing six clients a week for half that time. An important factor in determining how successful the outcome will be is how you connect with the counsellor, and the initial conversation you have with them can be helpful in this regard.

If you are working, you may need to find out if the counsellors have evening vacancies or whether they see people at weekends. Finally, ask what their charges are. Expect to pay between £30 and £45 a session. There may be a higher charge for an initial session which includes an assessment (although, paradoxically, some counsellors may offer a first session free of charge). Therapists, who are recognized as being at the very top of their profession, may charge as much as £100 a session.

Although one-to-one counselling is probably the most common, difficulties sometimes arise within a relationship. In later years, troublesome teenagers, the "empty nest" syndrome when children leave home, or the onset of retirement can all put a strain on previously stable families. In any of these situations, you and a partner may feel the best approach would be to see someone together. If so, make sure the counsellor is thoroughly experienced in this area, as the skills involved in seeing two people are much more than simply an extension of counselling an individual. The agency Relate, which has branches all over the country, specializes in counselling for any two people living together in a close relationship.

Some therapists also undertake telephone counselling. This can provide an alternative for those who cannot easily get around. Also, some people prefer the relative anonymity of counselling over the phone. The disadvantage of this method of counselling is that with only one element of communication in place, the therapeutic relationship may not be able to develop as effectively as when both client and counsellor are sharing the same space. Subtle changes in body language, and facial expression both in individual sessions and over the longer term can be very informative, particularly as these are often involuntary.

At times of emotional emergency, however, the need to speak to someone may be too urgent to go through the usual channels of finding a counsellor. Samaritans, for example, man crisis telephone hotlines 24 hours a day.

Finally, there is group therapy. Unlike private counselling, the essence of group therapy is one of shared experience. The group usually consists of six to eight people and provides a safe setting in which members can talk about difficulties in their lives and how they coped. Finding that a particular problem may be shared by others can do much to offset a person's sense of isolation or inadequacy. An important aspect of this form of therapy is that no one is obliged to take part, so people can join in as their confidence increases.

CHAPTER ELEVEN

What qualifications should a counsellor have?

SURPRISINGLY, there is presently no legal requirement for someone advertising themselves as a counsellor to have any qualifications. The Health Professions Council, (HPC) the government body that could be responsible for licensing counsellors, does not presently have a category for them. The HPC is currently in discussion with The British Association of Counselling and Psychotherapy (BACP) and other organizations to draw up the criteria for counsellors to be licensed. But there is a strong body of opinion contending that psychotherapy is not a branch of medicine and that, in any event, the HPC is not the right regulator for the job.

In practice, this is not really a problem as reputable therapists belong to one or other of the recognized professional counselling bodies, all of which have strict codes of ethics. These set out in fine detail the standards and responsibilities to which their members must adhere when counselling their clients. Counselling organizations have their own websites which specify the requirements of membership and conduct. Proof of registration can be obtained from the establishment of which counsellors say they are a member.

Because the concept of talking therapies may seem relatively straightforward, it might be thought that it doesn't take too much to train to be a counsellor. But this is not the case, and rightly so. Counsellor training is not dissimilar to that of other branches of the healthcare professions and requires a significant commitment of time, effort and money. To achieve a diploma, counsellors will have had to undergo some three years of hard work.

Initially, counsellors typically go on a short induction course designed to acquaint them with the whole philosophy of psychotherapy, and the disciplines, both personal and professional, they will have to master.

The primary aim is to enable them to decide whether this is a career to which they are suited and wish to pursue.

If they opt to continue after the induction course, the next stage is to obtain a Certificate in Counselling, which usually takes about a year of part-time college attendance with a variety of assignments to complete between classes. This is a practical course of instruction in techniques and skills, and serves as an introduction to the wide range of approaches to counselling, (of which more in a later chapter). The course gives trainee counsellors the opportunity to decide which way of working best suits their particular temperaments and life experience. Many will attend other courses in parallel with the certification course to increase their understanding of their chosen modality or their overall knowledge of the mental health environment. Some will have counselling themselves so they can work through personal issues and learn what it's like to be a client.

After obtaining their Certificate, counsellors move on to study for their diploma, which is often part of a university curriculum. Diploma courses normally take two years of part time study and practical learning, coupled with a considerable amount of homework and exams at intervals. Students are required to be in continuous training outside the faculty and to obtain experience as a placement with a counselling agency, usually as a volunteer. Failure to pass any exam stage usually means relegation or termination of the course. Course time will be at least 400 hours, with homework on top, and overall expenditure can easily be some £10,000–£12,000.

With the award of a diploma, which will reflect their specialty, the counsellor reaches professional status. Some will stay on in further education to obtain an MA or MSc in their chosen modality. Most counselling organizations have an accreditation process which recognizes the member's skills and adherence to their criteria for continuing professional development and continuity of practice.

Continuing professional development, often referred to as CPD, plays an important part in ensuring counsellors maintain their skills. Psychotherapy, like other branches of healthcare, is constantly evolving. Some psychological conditions, such as Asperger's syndrome, a mild form of autism, have been fully recognized and quantified only relatively recently. There are many other conditions such as ADHD (Attention Deficit Hyperactivity Disorder), and ODD (Oppositional Defiant Disorder), not to mention CM (Catastrophic Misinterpretations)! Elements of these and other psychological syndromes, many of which soon get reduced to acronyms, often present directly or indirectly in counselling. As such, they need to be recognized and their implications understood.

Even if they don't use them in their own practice, counsellors also need to know about new assessment and treatment techniques such as EMDR (Eye Movement Desensitizing and Reprocessing), used to help people like refugees who have undergone severe emotional shock.

Drugs used to treat chronic anxiety and depression may have a major impact on how a client presents, and counsellors' should have an understanding of the clinical and psychological responses to these agents.

Counsellors need to know of the availability of agencies or government bodies that may be able to offer further support for their clients, such as the Citizens Advice Bureau or organizations offering shelter in cases of abuse. They should also have knowledge of relevant local and national benefit schemes.

To enable counsellors to stay up to date, universities, colleges and counselling organizations offer a range of workshops and seminars throughout the year. These give therapists opportunities to refine their skills and benefit from the experiences of colleagues. Some counselling agencies set aside funds specifically so their members can attend such courses.

CHAPTER TWELVE

Do all counsellors work the same way?

THERE ARE NUMEROUS counselling approaches. Very often these share the same origin, but elements of them have been extended or modified by individual psychoanalysts or therapists until a new version of the technique becomes sufficiently structured and recognisable to be given a title of its own.

Broadly speaking there are three methods of counselling.

The first of these is the Freudian related therapies. Counselling, as we recognize the term, began with the work of Sigmund Freud who founded the psychoanalytical approach in the mid-nineteenth century. Freudian theorists argue that adult problems can be traced to unresolved conflicts from certain phases of childhood and adolescence. Freud promoted the idea of free association in which individuals are invited to relate whatever comes into their minds during the session. This technique, called psychoanalysis, is intended to help the person learn more about what he or she thinks and feels in a non-judgmental atmosphere. Free association has no pre-planned agenda, but works by intuitive leaps and linkages, which may lead to new insights and meanings. Neither therapist nor subject knows in advance exactly where the session will lead. Freud's work was further developed by Carl Jung, who explored the human psyche through the worlds of dreams, art, mythology, religion, and philosophy.

An approach practiced by many counsellors in this country is psychodynamic therapy, which stems directly from Freud's and Jung's pioneering work. Like psychoanalysis, psychodynamic therapy draws on the theory that childhood experiences have created or contributed to our current patterns of thinking and behaviour. It argues that we develop defences to protect ourselves from unhappy early experiences and memories because their impact would be too disruptive to carry forward into adult life. This often leads to denial, as emotions, feelings, and thoughts become repressed and manifest themselves as anxiety, guilt, or other negative symptoms.

Psychodynamic therapy sets out to help us rediscover these unconscious memories so that we can better understand them. The assumption is that once we know what they are, we are in a much better position to deal with them and put them into perspective.

This approach may particularly appeal to people who are interested in the workings of the human mind and who are prepared to accept that negative events in their past could colour their whole lives. Psychodynamic counselling can be very effective, but tends to be a long-term commitment.

The person-centred or humanistic therapies constitute the second main branch of counselling. They have their origin in the work of an American psychologist, Carl Rogers. Rogers wanted to move away from the analytical focus of the Freudian approach. He worked from a basis that human beings have an innate capacity for positive self-regard and, as such, are capable of moving forward on their own without having to rely on the counsellor to give their lives meaning. He likened people who were unable to realize their potential to a plant stored in a dark cellar with a small window trying to spread its tendrils towards the light. If the plant is moved into the right environment to permit healthy growth it will, without prompting, do just that. He believed that we know best who we are, and that in a supportive environment we are capable of positive change.

Rogers emphasized the importance of empathy in which the counsellors develop the skill to put themselves in their clients' shoes so as fully to understand what they are feeling. He developed the concept of non-judgmental, unconditional positive regard and genuineness. If the therapist demonstrates these qualities, argued Rogers, the client will improve, even if no other techniques are used.

Humanistic counselling has been criticized on the grounds that it is an art or philosophy rather than a form of treatment, and that it lacks predictive power. As such, it is rather disregarded by the NHS. Nevertheless, whilst hard evidence may not be available, all modalities endorse Rogerian criteria in recognizing the importance of empathy and unconditional acceptance as being fundamental to the development of successful client/counsellor relationships.

The third major branch of counselling comprises the behavioural therapies, which include Cognitive Behavioural Therapy (CBT), and Rational Emotive Behaviour Therapy (REBT).

At the heart of cognitive therapies is the idea that our responses to events or interpretations of experiences are based on beliefs we have about what they mean to us, rather than the events themselves. The Roman philosopher, Epictetus observed: "Men are disturbed not by things, but their view of things". Where these "views" are rigid or extreme we may make demands of ourselves, the world, or other people, which are unrealistic and illogical, so inducing anxiety, depression or other unhealthy emotions.

To take a simple example: suppose two people—we'll call them Bill and Ben—are going for a driving test. They have pretty much the same level of skills and will be assessed by the same examiner, going over the same route. Bill really wants to pass as he has been offered a job if he does. He will be very disappointed if he fails, and won't enjoy telling his prospective employer he can't take the job, but he knows there's no guarantee he'll get through first time; people often don't. He sets out determined to do his best. If he doesn't pass, he accepts he'll just have to take more lessons.

The driving test is also important to Ben. Like Bill, there is a job waiting for him if he gets through. But Ben insists to himself he absolutely *must* pass. This demand is driven by the belief that it would be unbearably humiliating to have to tell his prospective employer he couldn't take the job. Not surprisingly, in this frame of mind, Ben sets out to take his test in a state of high anxiety. Despite his seemingly greater drive to get through, he may be less likely to come away with a pass.

The objective of CBT and REBT is therefore to help clients recognize forms of thinking which produce unhealthy emotions and behaviour, and to explore alternatives which give them more flexibility and a higher level of tolerance.

However, it is well recognized that there is a considerable difference between accepting the concept of a more productive way of thinking and putting this changed thinking into effect. So an important aspect of cognitive therapies is the negotiation of between-session assignments designed to help clients put their new beliefs into practice.

Other modalities include Transactional analysis (TA), developed in the 1960s by the psychiatrist Eric Berne. TA is concerned with relationships. It is modelled on the idea that we all have three parts or "ego-states" to our personality: Parent, Child and Adult, each with their own subtleties, and that we converse or "transact" with one another in one of these forms. Adult to Adult and Child to Parent or Parent to Child transactions are generally smooth and productive.

Problems arise when lines are crossed. When someone addresses us as an Adult, we may decide to respond by playing the submissive (or rebellious) role of the Child. This can throw the first person into adopting an authoritarian or overly caring role of a Parent. Berne recognized that people often deliberately deploy crossed versions of these ego states to manipulate others. He famously encapsulated this theory in his entertaining book *Games People Play* which has sold over a million copies. Counsellors will often use clients' reproduction of dialogue with their partners or their colleagues at work to explore whether such crossed lines may be present.

Gestalt therapy, an approach developed by the German psychiatrist, Fritz Perls, explores the whole of a person's experience; thoughts, feelings, and bodily sensations with the aim of helping them be more aware of who they are. The expectation is that as different aspects of the self come into awareness, it enables the development of more fulfilling relationships and a freer way of functioning in the world.

One of the features of Gestalt therapy is role-playing. Practitioners often use a "two chair" technique in which the client is invited to move from one seat to the other as she or he engages in a dialogue between parts of themselves, or with other people. This enables them to act out and explore relationships, and so acquire a better insight into their behaviour and thinking.

This is by no means a complete list. Other therapeutic styles are continually evolving as alternatives to, or improvements on exist-ing ways of counselling, but they all have the same objective; to help people lead more self-fulfilling lives. As such, they share common features.

For example, in line with the person-centred approach to therapy, all counsellors, what-ever their orientation, will seek to establish a non-judgmental, empathic relationship with their clients, based on unconditional acceptance, as they recognize this is fundamental to the success of any work they do.

In the same way, although cognitive therapists primarily focus on the here and now, they certainly do not discount the past. They recognize that events taking place earlier in life need to be addressed if unhelpful beliefs they generated are being carried forward into the present. Equally, psychodynamic therapy whilst focusing initially on the client's past, takes fully into consideration the present day effects of counter-productive memories from childhood.

CHAPTER THIRTEEN

What should I expect from a counsellor?

COUNSELLORS ARE TRAINED in a number of techniques to create and maintain a productive environment and to deploy the interpretative skills that will enable them to evaluate what their clients are telling them. These skills may not be overtly evident, but if any of them are lacking it will soon be seen to have an adverse effect on the counselling relationship.

Before counselling begins, the therapist should seek your informed consent to proceed. This is not just a matter of your agreeing to have counselling—that's a given—but of ensuring you have an understanding of how the counsellor you've chosen works. Although all approaches have the same objective, there are many ways of setting out to achieve this, as shown in the previous chapter. Some processes, such as CBT, are primarily aimed at problem solving; other techniques may be more concerned with revealing the significance of events from our early years and exploring how these may still be influencing our thoughts and behaviour today. For these reasons, it can be useful when first making contact with a counsellor to find out how they like to work, particularly in relation to the issues you will be bringing with you.

If you are going to discuss very personal matters with someone, you will want to be sure a number of factors are in place. The first of these is that everything you talk about will be kept in the strictest confidence. This is a fundamental undertaking required by all counselling organizations and your therapist should assure you on this point before work begins.

The second is the provision of a private, neutral but comfortable setting, with chairs arranged so that you can look at one another, but not face-to-face which can feel confrontational. If the room seems too hot or too cold, it is sensible to say so. The counsellor will certainly try to accommodate you, for the fewer the distractions, the better. Some counsellors work from home, but you should not find yourself sitting in a room with pictures of their family on display or other evidence of their personal tastes, since information about the therapist has no relevance to the business in hand. Still less should there be an active telephone in the room, since the possibility of any intrusion is to be avoided.

The third essential is that you will get their full attention. Counsellors are trained in active listening skills so that they can focus on what they are hearing, evaluate the information you provide and seek clarification where need be without being sidetracked by unusual accents or different ethnic backgrounds.

Inactive listening: not recommended

They take into account your body language; how comfortable you seem to be when talking; for example, whether you are perched on the edge of the chair or sitting back. Unconscious repetitive movements also contribute to the information the counsellor draws upon to build up a picture of what is happening and the significance of certain elements of what is being said. Counsellors analyse factual information for the emotional content it may contain and will reflect back to you their interpretation of what they think you are telling them. Such reflections can also be helpful in enabling you to hear your ideas expressed by someone who does not colour the playback with their own prejudices.

The fourth element is for the counsellor to provide sufficient time and space for you to talk about why you have come for counselling. It is essential you be able to go at your own pace without feeling you have to rush through before the other party starts to show other signs of impatience or interrupts, as perhaps might occur with a friend or family member.

This aspect is important for counsellors too, since a hurried exposition may result in salient details being omitted, so presenting a false or inadequate picture which could seriously hold back or divert their understanding of what needs to be addressed.

A fifth factor is the counsellor's unconditional acceptance of you as you are. It is vital that you be able to talk in a non-judgemental atmosphere, otherwise there is a risk you'll instinctively withhold information that you might feel shows you in a bad light or engenders disapproval. Counsellors are disciplined to set aside personal views on factors such as gender, race, lifestyle, culture and sexual orientation so that their clients have an impartial, secure and supportive environment in which to bring up the issues they want to talk about.

An important component of the relationship between counsellor and client is the observance of boundaries. Boundaries provide a formal framework for the therapeutic process and define the arrangement between you. For example, you need to be confident that the counsellor will be there for you on the stated days, and times. You need also to be sure that you are agreed on the duration and number of sessions and the fee paid for them. You should feel confident, too, that there will be no impropriety. The observance of boundaries also means that counsellors should not put their own needs or interests ahead of those of their clients.

As mentioned in an earlier chapter, there are a number of ways in which counselling engages with problems that clients bring to them.

Counsellors should be able to describe the philosophy behind their approach in plain, nontechnical language even at the time of your first enquiry. Some will say that, whilst following a particular school of therapy, they are "eclectic", or "integrative", meaning they will draw on a variety of techniques from other modalities on an as-needed basis. In fact, most counsellors do this to some extent, whatever their orientation as they are initially trained to understand all the principal modes of counselling.

As counsellors do not bring their own agendas to sessions they will usually be reluctant to talk about themselves. The therapist's job is to understand the client not to obtain the client's understanding of their own situation. If counsellors start talking about their difficulties or personal preferences, the therapy changes to a mutual relationship, as with a friend. That said, revelation of a specific shared experience, can be supportive in providing evidence of the counsellor's understanding or simplifying an explanatory process.

Your counsellor should advise you that he or she has "supervision". This is a mandatory requirement specified by all professional counselling organizations. Supervision is a slightly unfortunate term, since it implies that someone else is in charge and telling the counsellor what to do. This is not the case. Supervision exists because resolving the issues that clients bring to counselling is rarely straightforward. With perhaps several avenues to pursue, it can be helpful for counsellors to discuss these in general terms with a qualified, experienced professional not immediately involved with the situation. Supervisors do not instruct counsellors, although they may make suggestions if they are concerned about an aspect of the management of a case. Although supervisors are themselves bound to confidentiality, counsellors do not reveal unnecessary information concerning the identity of their clients.

Finally, counsellors should be able to recognize where a situation falls outside their range of experience or where their approach to therapy is not producing results. In such cases they should be willing and able to make a judicious referral to a colleague whose qualifications may better match the client's needs.

CHAPTER FOURTEEN

What happens in a counselling session?

THIS DEPENDS, at least in part, on your counsellor's way of working. It is useful to have some idea of his or her orientation before you start, as whilst all approaches share the common aim of helping you to move forward, they do so in different ways. These were reviewed in an earlier chapter.

Unless someone else has already done an assessment, as happens with agencies, at the start of the initial session the counsellor will likely begin by asking you some questions about your background and family history. This is so that when you talk about the issues that have brought you to counselling, he or she will be able to decide how best to address your concerns.

"Now Mr Smith,
what seems to be the problem?"

Events in childhood can have a significant effect on our outlook on life even if we haven't realized it. Was our family close or were our parents separated? Who brought us up? Whom did we look upon as the most important influence in our early years? Was our childhood happy?

Do we have siblings and if so, how did we get on, and do we remain in contact? Even questions about how we spend our leisure time can provide useful material. Factors like the death of a close relative, an experience of violence or abuse, or alternatively a successful career move, or embarking on a new relationship can affect, sometimes profoundly, how we think of life at any given time.

The counsellor is also likely to ask if their client has had previous counselling, has ever stayed in a psychiatric hospital, and is currently on any medication. He or she will also want to ensure that they will be in a position to help. If there is a likelihood that a client has serious suicidal tendencies, a life-threatening illness, which they have not revealed to anyone else, or if they are prone to acts of extreme violence when they feel provoked, the counsellor may recommend psychiatric or medical care.

The counsellor's objective is also to ensure that he or she is aware of any factors that could influence progress so that these can be given due consideration and weight.

Once the assessment is complete, the therapist will be in a position to invite you to talk about why you have decided to come for counselling. Aware that it can be stressful discussing intimate aspects of one's life with a stranger, the counsellor will seek, as a priority, to establish a therapeutic alliance, since the way you connect with one another is likely to determine how successful therapy will be.

What you will instinctively be looking for in your counsellor is empathy. This is not the same as sympathy or pity. We can feel compassion for another person who is in a bad way or sorry for someone who has sustained a loss without necessarily becoming involved.

Empathy is described as the ability to communicate understanding of another person's experience from that person's world through their eyes without forfeiting one's own sense of reality.

In recognition of the difficulty that people sometimes experience in trying to find the right language to express themselves, or to bring to the surface childhood traumas, which might be quite deeply buried, some counsellors may provide aids to help the process. These can be in the form of a table with a range of objects; miniature dolls, toys, plasticine, crayons and paper that clients can use or arrange to create metaphors of their deeply held feelings.

At the end of the hour the counsellor is likely to ask how you felt the session went. One's instinct here might be to be polite, but if you do have concerns it is important you voice these. The counsellor should welcome your comments as it is useful to know if there are aspects of the way they have been working that are troubling you, since he or she then has a chance of addressing them. This may not be done if nothing is said.

You may in due course agree on between-session assignments or activities that will enable you to try out and practice new ways of thinking or productive behaviour. Any difficulties you encounter can be the subject of the following session. The more specific the agenda you bring, the more effectively the time can be used.

CHAPTER FIFTEEN

What should
I contribute
to the process?

THE CLASSIC FREUDIAN picture of the patient lying on a couch and talking about whatever comes into his mind whilst the analyst sits out of sight behind him, often saying nothing, is not the way counselling is usually practiced now. An active relationship between client and counsellor is generally considered fundamental to the success of therapy, regardless of the way the counsellor works.

The first essential is for you to know what you want to achieve from counselling. This should be reasonably specific, but also realistic. Going in with the requirement of, say, "wanting to feel happy" is rather too woolly to provide a focus. Happiness may come as a consequence of something we do or strive to do, but is not an entity that can be achieved in a vacuum.

Goals such as "I want to deal with my feelings of anxiety whenever I find I'm on my own" or "I want to be able to control my anger when I'm criticized" enable the therapist to explore with you how your feelings of loneliness developed or the circumstances that may bring out your anger.

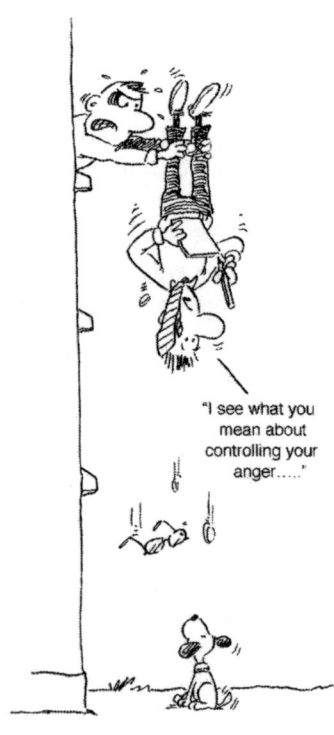

"I see what you mean about controlling your anger....."

Secondly, it is clearly important that you discuss fully and frankly the factors that are causing you problems. For you to do this, you need to be confident that your counsellor will give you unbiased, non-judgmental attention, and that he or she recognizes the validity of what, for you, are troublesome issues. This is why the establishment of trust is so fundamental to the counselling relationship. If you don't feel the counsellor is taking you seriously or are concerned that the environment may not be safe, it is hardly likely that you will take the difficult step of revealing highly personal aspects of your life.

Thirdly, always bear in mind that the essence of counselling is not for the therapist to tell you what to do, but to enable you to find your own solutions to the problems you are experiencing. Part of this process involves the counsellor inviting you to consider or reconsider aspects of your thinking which you may have come to believe reflect reality, but which in fact could be derived from your interpretation of events, past or present. An essential requirement is for you to bring an open mind to the process, so that you can give new ideas unbiased consideration, even if your instincts initially rebel against the implications that a change of philosophy may bring.

It can be helpful to think of oneself as taking part in a journey, which is sometimes called "guided discovery". You are doing the discovering and the counsellor is providing the guidance.

One of the harder aspects of counselling is that often we may feel worse before we feel better. This can happen at the stage where we recognize the benefits of changing our thinking but do not yet have the skills to put these changes into effect.

This is where the fourth element comes in; stamina to stay the course, and tolerate the discomfort that comes with knowing what you have to do but recognizing that you are not yet able to do it. The progress from understanding a concept in principle to the enactment of practical skills to bring it about requires commitment and hard work. If you confine your efforts only to the period you are in the counselling room, you'll be seeing your therapist for a very long time.

This need for stamina is directly connected to the fifth element—continuity. You will have appreciated that counselling isn't a magic bullet, and to get the full benefit it is essential to commit to regular, usually weekly, sessions. If the continuity is broken, the impetus to move forward is no longer sustained and you risk drifting back to the default position you are trying to move away from.

Finally, a note of caution. It sometimes happens that a friend or colleague tells you that a form of therapy they have been having, often one of the less conventional approaches, is doing them wonders, has changed their lives, improved their health, their appetite, or their skills at doing crosswords. If they are convincing enough, you may be tempted to give their practitioner a whirl alongside your existing counsellor on the grounds that two bites at the cherry could be better than one. But generally this is not a good idea. Almost inevitably you will end up with contradictory feedback. At any session, you may spend more time unpicking what the other therapist has been telling you than focusing on what is happening now, and this can leave you confused and uncertain as to how you are doing or the best way to move forward.

CHAPTER SIXTEEN

What might block my progress?

AS DISCUSSED EARLIER, although all therapists have the same objective, namely to enable you to develop your life skills, they set about this in one of a number of different ways. It may well be that a particular methodology doesn't work for you, in which case you could find yourself becoming frustrated and stuck. This is one reason why it is worthwhile checking with the counsellor how they work before starting. If you feel their approach might not be right for you, it may be better to look for someone else.

Major organizations, such as The British Association of Counselling and Psychotherapy, define the ethical framework for good practice in great detail, covering responsibilities to clients, the moral codes which counsellors should observe, and the overall quality of care they should provide. The vast majority of counsellors adhere closely to these guidelines and practice high standards of professional conduct. But you may feel uneasy for other, less immediately definable reasons; a sense of an innuendo, or a remark you may perceive as having erotic overtones.

Counsellors are not prohibited from touching their clients; indeed, a compassionate hand on an arm, even a hug can be appropriate in the right circumstances. But it is usually evident if this is well intentioned. In most respects, the boundaries of counselling are similar to those exercised by a doctor. You would not expect your GP to be drunk when you consulted him. Neither would you expect him to propose you meet socially, nor give you presents, nor make remarks suggestive of a sexual interest.

Reports do sometimes emerge of counsellors failing to meet these criteria. The counselling organizations take such breaches very seriously and if complaints are upheld, the therapist may be required to undergo further training or even have their membership withdrawn.

It is fair to say that infractions occur very infrequently. But, if you do feel uncomfortable with some aspect of your counsellor's manner or approach then you may want to relay your concerns to them. If he or she does not respond satisfactorily, it is usually best to follow your instincts and move away.

CHAPTER SEVENTEEN

How do I manage the effects of change?

C OUNSELLING IS ABOUT CHANGE, but no one changes in isolation. It's important to recognize that progress will not be even or regular. There will inevitably be times when you will drop back, but this does not mean you have gone all the way to the bottom again. This is a good reason for keeping some kind of journal when you are having counselling; a place in which you note your successes—and setbacks. This will help enable you to retain a sense of proportion and provide the evidence of what you have been able to achieve at those times when you feel you're not doing as well as you would wish.

The saying "No man (or woman) is an island" is well demonstrated in counselling. Your increasing independence and confidence can be hugely liberating, but it can also dramatically affect a relationship or the way you are perceived by others. This can sometimes be problematic.

If, for example, you came for counselling with the belief that you needed approval in order to feel valued, it is likely you will have been putting other people's interests ahead of yours in seeking to please them. If you free yourself of this belief, these same people could find your growing independence inconvenient or discomforting, and as a result, may seek to test your resolve in an effort to restore the status quo. If pressing your buttons no longer produces results, they will likely try harder before they finally accept that you have withdrawn your permission for them to do this. The process of inducing acceptance at home or at work that you have changed can therefore be quite taxing. Where close relationships may have been at risk, the other party may frustratingly insist on hard evidence over a period that the changes in your thinking and behaviour have a solid foundation.

But, like you, other people too can learn and as you are likely, through your counselling, to have developed a more flexible outlook on life, this should help the process along.

CHAPTER EIGHTEEN

What about online counselling?

A S MIGHT BE EXPECTED in a computer-driven age, counselling can now be accessed on self-help courses through the Internet. The modality presently best suited for this is Cognitive Behavioural Therapy (CBT) as it is a relatively structured approach. As such, it could be construed as being less dependant on a personal relationship with a counsellor. Although the service is free and approved by NICE, users have to register with their GP or health worker to sign up. They are given an activation code and their GP receives regular progress reports. It is still early days and to date only a very few practices have complied with official requirements to undertake the process.

Two such websites offering computerized CBT (cCBT) are Beating the Blues® <u>http://www.</u>

beatingtheblues.co.uk for the treatment of depression, and FearFighter http://www.fearfighter.com for panic and phobias. A third alternative, which does not involve a GP, is Living Life to the Full, http://livinglifetothefull.com a free, online life-skills course, again based on *CBT*. It is important to bear in mind that Internet counselling cannot replace the unique relationship between counsellor and client and that the person reviewing progress, whilst medically qualified, may not have therapist training.

Another approach to online support is through peer group befriending and mentoring. For this there is a website called Horsesmouth, set up on the basis that untapped wisdom is wasted. Horsesmouth invites those with the relevant knowledge and skills to offer the benefit of their experiences as mentors. For those accessing the website, there is the opportunity to seek guidance on a wide range of topics from general health and well being, through relationships and family matters, to choosing a career and managing problems at work.

Again, this is not a replacement for counselling. It is perhaps closer to an advice column in a newspaper or a radio panel programme in which experts on a subject answer questions phoned through to them. Unlike counsellors, mentors talk about their own lives and specifically tender advice, but the wide range of topics offers the chance to explore ideas and share other people's perspectives.

CHAPTER NINETEEN

What long-term results can I expect?

A S DISCUSSED IN EARLIER SECTIONS, the ultimate aim of counselling is to enable you to be your own therapist so that you can independently cope with difficulties that have arisen through irrational beliefs you may have adopted, or events from the past that you have realized are influencing your reactions and responses to situations now.

But you will need to bear in mind that you will probably retain a default position, which needs to be monitored, to avoid your assuming the attitudes and ways of thinking that caused you trouble in the first place. If you previously experienced road rage when another motorist pulled out in front of you, you will likely still experience some irritation when this happens. But, hopefully, you will not now feel the need to chase him for the next six miles until you can pull up in front of him and give him a piece of your mind!

Be aware that even with evident progress, you, as do all of us, will sometimes take two paces forward and one back—or even one pace forward and two back. The important thing is not to beat oneself up or despair when this happens. If one has been endeavouring in a matter of months to undo patterns of unproductive thinking acquired perhaps over many years, it is hardly surprising if one doesn't always maintain a steady pace. One of the objectives of counselling is to help us recognize situations, which could elicit unhealthy emotions and behaviour so that we can apply a constructive strategy to counter them before the old habits take hold.

As time goes on, this process should become more and more instinctive. Also, you will know that it is your responsibility how you think and behave, and nobody else's. Much as others may wish to impose their own ideas on us, there is no way they can do this without our permission. And that permission we have total authority to withhold!

CHAPTER TWENTY

How does counselling end?

THAT'S IT! BETTER! I'M DONE! It's tempting to think that once we feel we are coping with our difficulties we can take off. But ending abruptly risks compromising the work you will have undertaken with your counsellor. Ideally, a planned programme of one or more closing sessions should be agreed so as to be sure the process is complete and to tie up any loose ends.

Even before a final ending, it can be helpful sometimes to take a short break so as to give yourself the opportunity to put into practice what you have learned during your sessions. This can be a rehearsal towards a final ending and allows you to return on an as-needed basis to assess progress or to deal with a specific aspect that may still be causing difficulties.

In any event, it is always useful to establish with your counsellor that you can come back for a further session or two if you later find yourself experiencing problems.

* * *

The ending of counselling brings us to the end of this book. I hope it has been useful in enabling you to decide whether this form of therapy could be helpful for you. It does require courage to take the first step, but if you have some understanding of how the system works and what to expect you should be much better placed to make an informed choice. If you decide to take the plunge, then I wish you every success.